GUIDELINES

CHANUKAH

GUIDELINES

Over Two Hundred
of the Most Commonly
Asked Questions about
CHANUKAH

Rabbi Elozor Barclay
Rabbi Yitzchok Jaeger

TARGUM/FELDHEIM

First published 2001
Copyright © 2001 by E. Barclay & Y. Jaeger
ISBN 1-56871-283-9

All rights reserved

No part of this publication may be translated, reproduced, stored in a retrieval system, or transmitted in any form or by any means, electronic, mechanical, photocopying, recording, or otherwise, without prior permission in writing from the copyright holders.

Please address any questions or comments
regarding these notes to the authors:
E. Barclay (02) 583 0914
Y. Jaeger (02) 583 4889
email: jaeger@barak-online.net

By the same authors:
GUIDELINES TO PESACH
GUIDELINES TO THE YOMIM NORAIM

Published by:
Targum Press, Inc.
22700 W. Eleven Mile Rd.
Southfield, MI 48034
E-mail: targum@netvision.net.il
Fax toll free: (888) 298-9992

Distributed by:
Feldheim Publishers
200 Airport Executive Park
Nanuet, NY 10954
www.feldheim.com

Printed in Israel

הרב רפאל צבי ובר
רב דקהילת קמניץ
ונוה יעקב מזרח, ירושלים

י"ט אלול תשס"א
בס"ד

מכתב ברכה

שמחתי לראות קונטרס הלכות בשפה האנגלית שיצא לאור ע"י ידידי הרב ר' אלעזר ברקלי שליט"א והרב ר' יצחק ייגר שליט"א, והנני מכירם ויודעם בהשתדלות לאסוקי שמעתתא אליבא דהלכתא.

והנני מברכם שיקבלו דבריהם בביהמ"ד.

בברכת התורה,

צבי ובר

Rabbi Nachman Bulman
Yeshivat Ohr Somayach
Beit Knesset Nachliel

רב נחמן בולמן
מנהל רוחני ישיבת אור שמח
רב ק"ק נחליאל נוה יעקב מזרח

בע"ה

יום א', א' דראש חודש, ל' מנחם אב תשס"א פה עיה"ק ת"ו

Sunday, thirtieth of Menachem Av, 5671, the holy city of Yerushalayim.

I was delighted to see the third volume of the **Guidelines** series. The question and answers in **Guidelines** provide a clear and easily understood format and clarify relevant halachic issues.

It is clear from the quality of this work that Rabbi Elozor Barclay and Rabbi Yitzchok Jaeger have invested great amounts of time and effort in their thorough investigation of these dinim. Every answer has been written carefully and thoughtfully, considering both the classic and the most up-to-date halachic authorities. The accurate Hebrew references will certainly be an invaluable aid for any reader who wishes to investigate further.

I highly recommend this book to any person who is truly searching to know the correct conduct.

Signed with admiration,

נחמן בולמן

מנהל רוחני ישיבת אור שמח
רב ק"ק נחליאל נוה יעקב מזרח ביום הנ"ל
ועיני נשואות לשמים להסכמת שוכן במרומים

RABBI ZEV LEFF
Rabbi of Moshav Matisyahu
Rosh Hayeshiva Yeshiva Gedola Matisyahu

בס"ד
י"ח אלול תשס"א

It is with great pleasure that I received the manuscript of "**Guidelines**" to Chanukah by Rabbi Elozor Barclay שליט"א and Rabbi Yitzchok Jaeger שליט"א.

As in their previous works in this series, they have once again masterfully gathered the many laws of Chanukah into a concise, well-structured and clear compendium. This work will be a guide to those who cannot learn these laws from the Hebrew sources. To those who do learn these laws from their source, this book will serve as an aid for review and clarity.

May Hashem Yisborach grant the authors the ability to continue this series on all of the Yomim Tovim and to expand to other areas of Jewish law.

With Torah blessings,

Rabbi Zev Leff

Table of Contents

	Page
Foreword	11
Chapter One: Introduction	13
Chapter Two: The *Menorah*, oil and wicks	19
Chapter Three: Who is Obligated to Light a *Menorah*	23
Chapter Four: Where to Light	28
Chapter Five: When to Light	36
Chapter Six: Lighting the *Menorah*	43
Chapter Seven: Lighting Away from Home	53
Chapter Eight: Lighting in Shul	58
Chapter Nine: *Erev Shabbos*	63
Chapter Ten: *Motzai Shabbos*	69
Chapter Eleven: Prayers on *Chanukah*	71
Glossary	75
Index	78
Hebrew Sources	84

Foreword

With praise and gratitude to *Hashem Yisborach* we present a basic guide to the laws of *Chanukah*. Our first two books on the laws of *Pesach* and the *Yomim Noraim* were warmly received by the public, encouraging and motivating us to develop this third volume.

Once again we would like to state that one should not rely on these notes alone for a conclusive ruling and any doubts should be discussed with one's local *rav*. Our primary intent is to guide the reader through the maze of laws and customs which abound during this joyous period of the Jewish year, hence the title GUIDELINES.

The *halachos* of the *chagim* are numerous and complex and a person who is not familiar with them will certainly not be able to fulfill his obligation properly.

We would like to express our thanks to the *halachic* authorities who assisted in the preparation of this work. First and foremost we would like to express our appreciation to *HaGaon* Rav Nachman Bulman, *shlita*, whose decades of experience as a *posek* and community leader imbue this *sefer* with his invaluable perspective, reliablility and practicality.

We would also like to thank Rav Yitzchok Kaufman, *shlita*, who thoroughly checked the entire manuscript, providing many valuable corrections and observations.

Thanks are also due to Rabbi Moshe Dombey and all the staff at Targum Press who have once again demonstrated their professional expertise with the production of this book.

It is our hope that in the merit of keeping the laws of *Chanukah* punctiliously, we will all witness the dedication of the Third Temple, speedily in our days.

Elozor Barclay   Yitzchok Jaeger

Yerushalayim, Elul 5761

Chapter One
Introduction

1. What does *Chanukah* commemorate?

During the period of the second Temple, the Greek Empire took control of *Eretz Yisrael* and issued harsh decrees against the Jewish people. They forbade the study of Torah and the observance of *mitzvos*; plundered their possessions and violated their daughters; and entered the holy Temple damaging and desecrating it. When *Hashem* had mercy on His people, He saved them through the family of the *Chashmonaim Cohanim*. They miraculously defeated the Greek army, purified and rededicated the Temple, and reinstated the Jewish monarchy which continued for over 200 years until the destruction of the Temple.

2. Why do we light a *menorah*?

When the *Chashmonaim* entered the Temple and searched for pure undefiled oil to light the *menorah*, they found only one small bottle bearing the seal of the *Cohen Gadol*. Although this contained enough oil to burn for only one day, a miracle occurred and the oil sufficed for eight days until new pure oil was produced. The Sages therefore instituted the festival of *Chanukah* to rejoice and praise *Hashem* for eight days. Each evening a *menorah* is lit by the doors and windows of Jewish homes to show and publicize the miracle.

3. Why are these days called *Chanukah*?

- The word represents חנו כ"ה – they rested from their enemies on the 25th. The day on which the *Chashmonaim* defeated the Greeks was the 25th of *Kislev* (3597).
- The word means dedication, commemorating the rededication of the Temple by the *Chashmonaim*. Furthermore the building of the *Mishkan* was also completed on the same date – 25th *Kislev*.

4. How is *Chanukah* commemorated during *davening*?

The entire *Hallel* is recited every day and the additional praise *al haNissim* is inserted in *Shemoneh Esrei* and *bensching* (see chapter eleven). The Torah is read every day in shul and *tachanun* and *lamnatzeach* are omitted.

5. Why are there differences between the festivities of *Chanukah* and *Purim*?

Although one is required to have a festive meal on *Purim*, there is no such requirement on *Chanukah*. The reason for the difference is that *Haman's* decree was to physically annihilate the Jewish people, therefore the miraculous rescue is celebrated with physical festivities. However, the evil decrees of the Greeks were aimed at the spiritual destruction of the Jewish people. Had they forsaken the Torah and adopted Greek culture ח"ו these decrees would have been withdrawn. Therefore the miraculous defeat of the Greeks is celebrated in a spiritual manner, through praising and thanking

Hashem for enabling us to continue performing *mitzvos*.

6. Why do many people have festive meals?

According to some opinions, there is a *mitzvah* to have festive meals to celebrate the rededication of the Temple. In order for such a meal to be considered a *seudas mitzvah*, one should sing *zemiros* and praises to *Hashem* and talk about the great miracles. Unfortunately, some people misuse these occasions, wasting their time with card playing and other frivolities.

7. May a mourner join such a meal?

A mourner may participate in such a gathering if only family members are present.

8. Why do some people eat *latkes* and doughnuts?

It is a custom to eat foods fried in oil in order to remember the miracle of the oil that burned for eight days.

9. Why do some people eat milk dishes?

It is a custom to eat milk dishes in order to recall the miracle that took place through cheese. One of the evil decrees was that a Greek officer violated every engaged girl before her wedding. *Yehudis*, the daughter of *Yochanan Cohen Gadol* fed the commanding officer cheese and wine until he fell into a deep sleep. She then cut off his head and when the Greeks realized that their leader was dead, they fled.

10. Is one allowed to fast on *Chanukah*?
It is forbidden to fast, even if one has *Yahrzeit* for a parent. A bride and groom do not fast on their wedding day.

11. What is the origin of the *dreidel*?
During the Greek persecution, the Jews who wished to continue studying Torah had to do so in hiding. When the Greek officers approached, the Jews brought out games to play such as the *dreidel*. The letters on the *dreidel* נ, ג, ה and ש stand for נס גדול היה שם – a great miracle occurred there. Other deeper connotations can be found in these letters.

12. Are there any other special *mitzvos* on *Chanukah*?
- There is a special *mitzvah* to give charity on *Chanukah* and in particular to support needy Torah students. In this way we recall the miraculous fall of the evil Greeks into the hands of the righteous adherents to the Torah. The widespread custom to give *Chanukah gelt* to children may have developed from this *mitzvah*.
- There is also a *mitzvah* to devote extra time to Torah study. This demonstrates the defeat of the Greeks who prevented Torah study by their evil decrees.

13. May one work on *Chanukah*?

All forms of work are permitted. Women though have a custom to refrain from work for a short time every evening, since they were instrumental in causing the miracle (see question 9).

14. When should women refrain from work?

From the time the *menorah* is lit for half-an-hour.

15. What type of work is forbidden?

There are different customs about this. The main custom is to refrain from heavy household chores such as laundering, house cleaning, ironing and sewing. In Jerusalem, some women also refrain from cooking.

16. What is the correct *b'racha* for *latkes*?

If they are made from grated potatoes the *b'racha* is בורא פרי האדמה, but if they are made from potato flour the *b'racha* is שהכל. If flour or matzo meal is added for binding, the *b'racha* is not affected.

17. What is the correct *b'racha* for doughnuts?

The *b'racha* is בורא מיני מזונות. [According to a minority opinion, if the dough contains only a little oil or eggs, and tastes similar to bread, the *b'racha* may be המוציא.]

18. Is there a limit on the quantity of doughnuts one may eat?

There is no restriction to the quantity of doughnuts that one may eat. [According to a minority opinion, one should not eat a quantity which would fill an average person since this may require the *b'racha* of המוציא.]

19. If the doughnuts are served at the end of a meal, do they require a *b'racha*?

- If one is still hungry they do not require a *b'racha*, since they are considered part of the meal.
- If one is basically full and eating the doughnuts as a pleasant dessert, there is a dispute as to the correct procedure and therefore the situation should be avoided. If this situation does arise, a *b'racha* is not made. Preferably, one should *bensch* and eat the doughnuts after the meal.

20. May one visit a cemetery on *Chanukah*?

Some have the custom not to go, since weeping and mourning is forbidden on *Chanukah*. If a person wishes to visit the grave of a parent after *shiva* or *sh'loshim* or on a *yahrzeit*, he should preferably go before or after *Chanukah*. It is permitted to visit the graves of *tzaddikim* during *Chanukah* since this does not usually cause weeping.

Chapter Two
The *Menorah*, oil and wicks

21. From which type of material should the *menorah* be made?

In order to enhance the *mitzvah*, one should try to obtain as beautiful a *menorah* as possible according to his ability. The order of preference for different materials is silver, copper, other metals, glass, wood and china.

22. Are any materials forbidden?

One may not use eggshells or hollowed out vegetables to make the *menorah*, since this disgraces the *mitzvah*.

23. Is the shape of the *menorah* important?

It is preferable that the lights stand in a straight line and all at the same height. Therefore, one should not buy a modern design *menorah* whose branches are in a staggered position or of differing heights.

24. How far apart should the branches be?

They should be sufficiently spaced that a distance of one thumb width (2cm) separates each light from the next. If the lights were too close to each other they would appear like a torch which is not valid. According to some opinions, a *menorah* does not appear like a torch and no minimum separation is required.

25. What if one has no *menorah* at all?

A *menorah* enhances the *mitzvah* but is not essential. A person wishing to light with oil could use several glasses or cups placed in a straight line. If candles are being used, they may be fixed in a row onto a tray or similar surface.

26. Does one need to *toivel* the *menorah*?

No, since this item has no direct connection to food.

27. Is it preferable to use oil or candles?

Oil is preferable since the miracle in the Temple happened with oil.

28. Are all types of oil suitable?

The most preferred type of oil is olive oil since the miracle happened with olive oil. If one cannot afford or obtain olive oil, one may use any other oil (or paraffin) which burns with a clear flame.

29. May some lights be lit with oil and some with candles?

No, one should not mix the two. All the lights should be either oil or candles. However one may use oil on one night and candles on another night. This is particularly relevant to a person who must travel during *Chanukah* and is unable to take an oil *menorah*.

30. Is solidified oil as good as liquid oil?

Since this melts as it burns, it is considered equally good.

31. If one uses oil but the wick is coated with wax is this considered lighting with oil?

Since the wax is part of the wick and melts immediately, it is considered as lighting with oil.

32. Does the oil require a *hechsher*?

Although the oil is only being burned and not eaten, nevertheless, one should buy oil with a *hechsher* since certain types are forbidden to use.

33. May one use oil which is bitter tasting and not fit to eat?

Since the oil is burned and not eaten this is permitted. According to some opinions, it is praiseworthy to use oil that can be eaten.

34. May one use oil that was left under a bed where someone slept?

It is preferable not to use such oil, unless nothing else is available.

35. Which type of wicks should be used?

All wicks may be used, but the most ideal is cotton wool or linen.

36. Should one use fresh wicks every night?

It is not necessary to replace the wicks every night. Some opinions prefer the reusing of wicks since they light better. Some have the custom to change the wicks every night in the same way that they were changed daily in the Temple.

37. May one throw away used wicks?

Since the wicks were used for a *mitzvah* one may not disgrace them by throwing them away in the garbage. One should burn them or wrap them in a bag before discarding them. (See question 146.)

38. May one use electric lights for the *menorah*?

Electric lights are not valid for the *mitzvah* of the *menorah*.

Chapter Three
Who is Obligated to Light a *Menorah*

39. Who is required to light a *menorah*?

According to the basic law it is sufficient to light one *menorah* per household, irrespective of the number of family members. However, the *Ashkenazic* custom is to beautify the *mitzvah* by each male member of the family lighting a separate *menorah*.

40. Are women required to light?

A woman living on her own is required to light a *menorah*. Although this is a time-bound *mitzvah*, women are obligated since they were included in the decrees and instrumental in the miraculous defeat of the enemy (see question 9).

41. If the father is lighting, can his daughters light their own *menorah*?

This is permitted, although the standard custom is not to do so. The reason is that originally everyone lit the *menorah* next to the doorway of the house in the street, and it was considered immodest for women to stand there among the crowds of men. Therefore they would stand in the house near the doorway and watch the men light. Although today many people light indoors, the custom remains. Even where daughters do have a custom to light their own *menorah*, the wife should not light since she is considered one unit with her husband.

42. Should children light?

The custom is to educate boys to light their own *menorah* from the age of six or seven. In families where daughters also light, one may allow girls of six or seven to light their own *menorah*, although there is no obligation to do so. Children should be given oil or candles that will stay alight for the required length of time (see questions 103 and 200).

43. What if the husband is out of town during *Chanukah*?

In this case, either the wife or a son over bar mitzvah should light the *menorah* on behalf of the family (see also question 151).

44. Is a boarder required to light his own *menorah*?

A person who permanently sleeps **and** eats with a family is considered as a member of the household and does not need to light his own *menorah*. According to the custom of '*mehadrin*', a male boarder should light his own *menorah*.

45. What if the boarder eats elsewhere?

A person who permanently sleeps with a family but usually eats elsewhere is not considered a member of the household and is not automatically included with them.

46. Where should such a boarder light the *menorah*?

• A man who regularly eats at one location should preferably light there. If this is difficult, he may light where he sleeps.

• If he does not regularly eat at one location, he should light where he sleeps.

• A woman who regularly eats at one location should preferably become a partner there. If this is difficult she may become a partner with the family where she sleeps.

• If she does not regularly eat at one location, she should become a partner with the family where she sleeps.

47. How does one become a partner with a family?

In order to become a partner one must acquire a share in the oil or candles. This can be done by giving a small amount of money to the host in order to purchase a share. Alternatively the host may give him a share as a gift, but in this case the lodger must lift up the oil or the candles as an act of acquisition. [According to some opinions, the host should add oil or use longer candles than usual.]

48. How much money must one give?
The value of an ancient coin called a *p'rutah*. Today this is a few *agurot* or a few cents (pennies).

49. Must one acquire a share every night?
No, it is sufficient to make the acquisition once on all the materials that will be used during *Chanukah*.

50. Who should light in a *Yeshivah*?
According to the custom of '*mehadrin*', each boy should light his own *menorah*. If this is difficult, several boys could become partners in one *menorah*. (See also questions 83, 84.)

51. Who should light in a seminary?
It is sufficient for one *menorah* to be lit on behalf of all the girls. The girls are automatically considered to be partners in the *menorah* if the oil or candles are bought with funds of the seminary. Ideally, the *menorah* should be lit by one of the students, or if necessary by one of the staff. A girl who wishes to be '*mehadrin*' and light her own *menorah* may do so.

52. Do all the partners in the *menorah* have to watch the lighting?
Yes, all the partners must be present at the lighting, since everyone over bar or bas mitzvah is obligated in the *mitzvah*. A person who is not actually lighting a *menorah* but is a partner with someone else must stand nearby and listen to the *brachos* being recited. The person who is lighting the *menorah* should have in

mind to include any partner with his *brachos*. This procedure is necessary in any of the cases mentioned above (e.g. wife, daughters, boarders, seminary students – see question 122).

53. What if one of the partners is not able to be present at the time of lighting?

His main obligation to light a *menorah* is fulfilled by the partner's lighting. However, according to some opinions, there is also an obligation to recite or listen to the *brachos*. Accordingly, he should make an effort to be present when a *menorah* is lit elsewhere. He should ask the person lighting to include him when reciting the *brachos* and he should answer 'amen'.

54. Who should light in a room shared by several girls?

They should become partners in a *menorah* by purchasing the materials together. Each night one girl should light the *menorah* in the presence of the others. A girl who wishes to be *mehadrin* and light her own *menorah* may do so.

Chapter Four
Where to Light

55. Where should the *menorah* be placed?

The most ideal place is outside a door of the house that faces the street, to publicize the miracle of *Chanukah* as much as possible. This is the prevalent custom in *Eretz Yisrael*.

56. Why is this not done in *chutz la'aretz*?

In *chutz la'aretz* the prevalent custom is to light the *menorah* indoors. Several reasons have been suggested for this:
- The gentiles may become antagonistic.
- The gentiles may extinguish or steal the *menorah*.
- The winter weather conditions of rain and strong winds do not make it practical to light outside.

57. How does one overcome the problem of winds in *Eretz Yisrael*?

The *menorah* should be placed inside a protective glass case. Although this involves extra expense, one is obliged to use such a case in order to fulfill the *mitzvah* properly.

58. Where outside the door should the *menorah* be placed?

If the door of the house is adjacent to the street, the *menorah* should be placed in the street outside the door. If there is a garden or yard between the street and the door of the house, there are two customs where to light. Some place the *menorah* in the street by the entrance to the garden or yard and some place it inside the garden or yard by the entrance to the house.

59. Must the entrance to the garden or yard have a doorframe?

No, any opening which has the form of an entrance may be used. One cannot light next to a completely open side of a garden, even if the garden is surrounded by walls on the other three sides.

60. On which side of the entrance should one light?

The *menorah* should be placed on the left side of the entrance within one hand-breadth of the doorpost (approx. 10cm). Since the *mezuzah* is on the right side, a person who enters the doorway will thereby be surrounded by *mitzvos*.

61. What if there is no *mezuzah* on the entrance (e.g. there is no complete doorframe)?

If there is no *mezuzah* on the entrance, the *menorah* should be placed on the right side.

62. What if it is difficult to place the *menorah* on the left side (e.g. there is a wall there)?

The *menorah* may be placed on the right side.

63. May one place the *menorah* in the space of the actual doorway?

Yes, the *menorah* may be placed in the space of the doorway on the left side (when there is a *mezuzah*).

64. In this case should the *menorah* be placed alongside the left doorpost or across the entrance?

If there is sufficient space, it is preferable to place it alongside the doorpost so that all the lights will be within a hand-breath of the wall. If this is impractical, the *menorah* may be placed across the entrance with its left branch close to the left doorpost.

65. What is the correct height of the *menorah*?

Ideally it should be placed so that the flame is above three hand-breaths from the ground (approx. 30 cm) and lower than ten hand-breaths (approx. 1m). This demonstrates that the *menorah* has been lit for a *mitzvah* only and not for illumination, since one does not usually place lighting so low.

Chapter Four – Where to Light

66. What if the *menorah* can not be seen from the street in such a low position?

In such a case the *menorah* should be placed at the height at which most people can see it, in order to create maximum publicity.

67. Is it preferable to place the *menorah* on the right of the door below ten hand-breaths or on the left of the door above ten hand-breaths?

The *menorah* should be placed in the position that is most visible to people in the street.

68. What if the *menorah* will not be seen from any position if it is placed next to the door?

The *menorah* should be lit inside the house by a window that can be seen from the street.

69. What if a person has neither a door nor a window that can be seen from the street?

The *menorah* should be placed on the left side of the doorway leading into the room that is most used during the evening.

70. If a person lives in an apartment block, where should he light?

This depends on the two customs mentioned earlier (see question 58).
- According to the first custom the *menorah* should be lit either in the street by the entrance to the

communal garden or yard, or by the door of the apartment block.
- According to the second custom it should be lit inside the house by a window that faces the street. If there is no window that faces the street but neighbors pass by his front door, the *menorah* should be lit there. Otherwise, see previous question.

71. May one light the *menorah* on the stairway outside the door of the apartment?

This is far from ideal and should be done only when there is no other alternative. Although the people living in the block will walk through the stairway and see the *menorah*, nevertheless this is not a public street and the publicity is minimal. It is considerably better to light the *menorah* by a window facing a street, or by an outside entrance.

72. If more than one person lights by an outside entrance how will people know who lit each *menorah*?

It is not necessary to know who lit each *menorah*. According to some opinions, only one person should light by the entrance and the others should light by a window facing the street, thereby publicizing the miracle in more locations.

73. Should everyone light on the left side or should some people light on the right?

If there is sufficient room, everyone may light by the left side.

Chapter Four – Where to Light

74. When should the *menorah* be placed by a window?

There are several possible situations:
- The entrance to the garden, yard or house is not visible from the street (see question 68).
- When living in an apartment block, according to the second custom (see question 70).
- In *chutz la'aretz* (see question 56).
- Another person already lit by the entrance to the building, according to one opinion (see question 72).

75. Which window should be chosen for lighting?

One should choose the window that enables the maximum number of people to see the *menorah*, since publicizing the miracle is an important part of the *mitzvah*.

76. Is it better to light by a bedroom or kitchen window that can be seen by many people or by a dining-room window that can be seen by fewer people?

It is better to light by the bedroom or kitchen window.

77. Does the height of the window matter?

If possible, the flames should be within ten hand-breaths (about 1m) from the floor of the house. If the *menorah* cannot be seen from the street at this height it should be placed higher (see question 66).

78. What about an upper floor window above street level?

One may certainly place the *menorah* by a window that is less than 20 cubits (about 11m) above the street since at this height it is easily visible. According to many opinions, it is permitted to light even above this height since the *menorah* is visible to people in the house, in nearby buildings and occasionally to people in the street. Some opinions disqualify a window that is higher than twenty cubits since the *menorah* is not easily noticed from the street. According to this opinion, the *menorah* should be lit next to the door of the house or of the building.

79. Where exactly by the window should one place the *menorah*?

On the right side of the window as one faces it.

80. May one light by a frosted window?

This is permitted even though the flames appear somewhat fuzzy from the street.

81. May several people light by the same window?

This is permitted on condition that the *menorahs* are spaced apart, so that one can easily see the number of lights in each *menorah*. If several suitable windows are available, it is preferable for each person to light by a different window.

Chapter Four – Where to Light

82. Should one light by a window if only gentiles will see the *menorah*?

There is a disagreement whether publicizing the miracle to gentiles is of any value. However, unless one is afraid of arousing antagonism, it is preferable to light by a window, since there is a possibility that a Jew may also see the lights.

83. Where should a *Yeshivah* student light?

- If he sleeps in the *Yeshivah* he should light there.
- If he sleeps at home or with a family it is preferable to light where he sleeps. However, if this will cause considerable disturbance to his learning schedule, he should light at the *Yeshivah*.

84. Where in the *Yeshivah* should he light?

- According to many opinions, he should light in his dormitory since this is designated for his personal use and is considered to be his home. It is praiseworthy to eat one or two meals each day in the bedroom (if possible).
- Others prefer the dining room since this is a more important place than a bedroom.
- According to a third opinion, he should light by the entrance to the *Yeshivah* dormitory, or by the entrance to the yard.
- In any event, students must consult with the staff before lighting anywhere in the *Yeshivah*, in order to avoid any inconvenience or risk of fire ח"ו.

Chapter Five
When to Light

85. When is the correct time to light the *menorah*?

There are two main customs:
- At sunset. This is the opinion of the *Vilna Gaon* and is widely accepted in *Eretz Yisrael*.
- At nightfall. This is the opinion of the *Shulchan Aruch* and is widely accepted in *chutz la'aretz*.

Some opinions suggest a compromise between these two opinions and recommend lighting ten to twenty minutes after sunset.

86. If a person lights at nightfall, should he *daven ma'ariv* first?

The main custom of those who light at nightfall is to *daven* immediately at nightfall and light after *ma'ariv*. However, it is preferable to light beforehand, even though it may be still before nightfall. A person who lights after *ma'ariv* should prepare the *menorah* beforehand and return home after *ma'ariv* without delay in order to light as early as possible.

87. What if a person intends to *daven ma'ariv* later in the evening?

According to some opinions, he should light the *menorah* immediately at nightfall. According to others, he should delay lighting the *menorah* until after *davening ma'ariv*. One should make an effort to *daven ma'ariv* on time during *Chanukah* in order to light the *menorah* at the correct time.

88. What if a person is unable to light at sunset or at nightfall?

If possible he should attempt to light within half-an-hour after nightfall. If this is not possible, he may light at any time during the evening.

89. What is the latest time for lighting?

One may light until *halachic* dawn.

90. May the *brachos* be recited when lighting late?

According to some opinions, one may only recite the *brachos* if some people are awake to see the lighting. However, the main custom is to recite *brachos* even if all the family is asleep.

91. What if the entire night passed without lighting?

The *mitzvah* has been lost and cannot be made up. On the next night he should light the same number as everyone else, even though he missed a night.

92. Is one permitted to light before sunset?

In extenuating circumstances when one will not be able to light later, one may light the *menorah* from *plag haMincha* (1¼ seasonal hours before sunset, see question 197). Care must be taken to ensure that the candles or oil will burn until half-an-hour after nightfall (see question 103). The *brachos* are recited as usual.

93. Is it preferable to light before sunset or late at night?

It is preferable to light late at night rather than before sunset.

94. What if a person is at work at the time of lighting?

In order to prevent people from lighting late, the Sages forbade engaging in work from half-an-hour before lighting time. Therefore, a person should ideally leave his place of work in order to light the *menorah* at home at the correct time.

95. Why are some people lenient about this?

Several reasons have been suggested to justify this lenient custom:
- According to most opinions, the ideal time to light nowadays extends beyond the first half-an-hour, since people are still in the street until late at night.
- Since many people (especially in *chutz la'aretz*) light indoors, the main publicity of the miracle is for the family members and this can be achieved even later in the evening.
- Leaving work early could cause a financial strain and possibly even a loss of one's job.

Nevertheless, a person who overcomes difficulties in order to fulfill the *mitzvah* properly will earn great reward. According to the Sages, whoever is punctilious with the *mitzvah* of kindling the *Chanukah* lights will be blessed with sons who are Torah scholars.

96. Does the work restriction apply to a person who is at home?

Yes. When a person is involved in various activities he may not notice the passage of time and the ideal lighting time may be missed. Therefore work must stop half-an-hour before sunset or nightfall (according to one's custom).

97. What type of activity is forbidden?

It is forbidden to start activities that
- take more than a few minutes **or**
- have a tendency to continue for some time **or**
- are hard to break off from in the middle.

Once the time has arrived, one must not engage in any activities whatsoever, and the *menorah* should be lit immediately.

98. Is Torah study also forbidden?

Torah study is permitted during the half-hour before lighting time and forbidden only when the actual time of lighting arrives.

99. May one eat or drink before lighting?

From half-an-hour before the time of lighting, one may not eat bread or cake more than the volume of an egg (approx. 60cc). There is no restriction on other foods or drinks during this period.

100. May one sleep before lighting?

This is certainly forbidden since there is a strong possibility that one may oversleep.

101. When would a person be permitted to work, eat or sleep before lighting?

If he appoints another person to remind him about the *mitzvah* of lighting, he is permitted to work, eat or sleep.

102. Do all these restrictions also apply to women?

These restrictions apply to any person who lights a *menorah*. Therefore, a woman who lives alone or whose husband is away must keep all the above restrictions. A woman who does not intend to light but fulfills her obligation with a man's lighting is not limited by the above restrictions.

103. For how long must the lights burn?

If one lights at nightfall or later they must be able to burn for at least half-an-hour. If one lights before nightfall, they must be able to burn until half-an-hour after nightfall.

104. Is it better for the lights to burn longer than this?

During the time of the Sages it was unusual for people to be on the street late at night. Therefore, there was little point in allowing the lights to burn for more than half-an-hour, since no one would see them. Today when people are still walking about in the street late at night, according to some opinions it is praiseworthy for the lights to burn longer. Using longer candles is in any case praiseworthy since this adds to the beauty of the *mitzvah*.

105. May one extinguish the lights after half-an-hour?

The widespread custom is to leave the lights to burn themselves out, especially in view of the opinions mentioned in the previous question. However, if it is necessary to extinguish the *menorah* (e.g. everyone is leaving and there could be a risk of fire ח"ו) one may do so.

106. What if the lights go out by themselves?

If sufficient oil or candles were placed in the *menorah* when it was lit, the *mitzvah* has been fulfilled, even if the lights went out within the required time. Although one is not obligated to rekindle the lights, it is correct to do so. This is particularly important on *erev Shabbos* when the *menorah* is lit much earlier than usual (see chapter nine). The *brachos* should not be repeated when re-lighting the *menorah*.

107. What if insufficient oil was put in the *menorah*?

If the *menorah* did not contain sufficient oil when it was lit, he has not fulfilled the *mitzvah*. He must extinguish the lights, add more oil and re-light them. However, the *brachos* should not be repeated.

108. What if there was sufficient oil but the wind blew out the lights?

If a person lights outside or near an open door or window, he must take precautions to prevent the wind from blowing out the lights. The standard procedure is to use a glass case. If despite this the wind blew out the lights, he is not obligated to re-light them, but it is correct to do so. If he kindled the lights in a windy place without taking necessary precautions, and they blew out, he has not fulfilled the *mitzvah*. The *menorah* should be put in a different location and re-lit, but without a *b'racha*.

109. What if the wicks are not catching fire properly?

If the wicks did not catch fire from the outset, he has not fulfilled the *mitzvah*. The wicks should be adjusted or replaced and the *menorah* re-lit immediately. The *brachos* should only be repeated if he was distracted from the *mitzvah*.

110. What if he tries to fix the wick while it is burning but he accidentally extinguishes it?

He is not required to re-light it, but it is correct to do so.

Chapter Six
Lighting the *Menorah*

111. How many lights are kindled each night?
According to the basic requirement, it is sufficient to kindle one light each night. However, the universally accepted custom is to beautify the *mitzvah* by kindling one light on the first night and adding an additional light each night, until eight lights are kindled on the eighth night.

112. What if a person cannot afford to buy sufficient oil or candles for such a procedure?
In such a situation he may fulfill the basic requirement of kindling one light each night.

113. Is it preferable to use oil but kindle only one light every night or to use candles but add one each night?
It is preferable to use candles adding one each night. This is a bigger enhancement of the *mitzvah* than kindling only one oil light each night.

114. Which end of the *menorah* should be used on the first night?
One should begin at the right end of the *menorah* as one faces it. This applies whether the *menorah* is

placed next to a doorway, inside a doorway or by a window.

115. What is the procedure on the subsequent nights?

Each night, an additional light is placed next to those of the previous night, gradually filling up the *menorah* towards the left. When lighting the *menorah*, the main custom is to kindle the newest light first, i.e. the left-most one and proceed to light from left to right.

116. Where exactly should one stand when lighting the *menorah* on subsequent nights?

It is incorrect to pass over the opportunity to do a *mitzvah*. Since the newest light is kindled first, one should stand close to it, i.e. slightly to the left of the lights. If he would stand to the right of the *menorah*, he would have to pass over the other lights before kindling the left-most first.

117. Why is an additional light, the '*shamash*', kindled?

The lights of the *menorah* are holy and one may not derive any personal benefit from them (see questions 135, 136). For this reason, an additional light is kindled called the '*shamash*' (service light), to be available for use when necessary. A *shamash* is required even if the electric lights are on.

118. Should one light the *shamash* before or after the main lights?

There are two customs.

- The main *Ashkenazic* custom is to light the *shamash* at the start before the *brachos* are recited. After reciting the *brachos*, the *shamash* is used for kindling the *Chanukah* lights and is then placed into the *menorah*.
- The main *Sephardic* custom is to use a different candle for lighting both the *Chanukah* lights and the *shamash*. According to this method, the *shamash* is placed on the *menorah* beforehand but only lit after the main lights. The candle used for lighting the *menorah* is then extinguished.

119. Should one use oil or a candle for the *shamash*?

- According to the *Ashkenazic* custom mentioned above, it is customary to use a candle for the *shamash* for practical reasons; it is much more convenient to kindle the lights with a candle than with an oil light.
- According to the *Sephardic* custom, one may use either a candle or oil for the *shamash*, since this light is not used to kindle the others.
- Some opinions recommend using a candle for the *shamash* if the main lights are oil, in order to make it clear that it is not included in the number of *Chanukah* lights.

120. Where should the *shamash* be placed?

The *shamash* should be placed away from the other lights, to distinguish it from them. If the *shamash* is close to the other lights it should be placed higher, but if this is difficult it may be placed lower. If candles are being used, one may use a longer candle for the *shamash*.

121. If several *menorahs* are lit does each one require a *shamash*?

Yes.

122. Must all the family watch the lighting?

Before beginning to light, the head of the household should call together all the members of the family to watch the lighting. There are two reasons for this:
- Those who do not light a separate *menorah* must fulfill the *mitzvah* by listening to the *brachos* of the person who lights (see question 52).
- There is greater publicity of the miracle when more people see the lights.

123. Which *brachos* are recited when kindling the *menorah*?

On the first night of *Chanukah* three *brachos* are recited:
- אשר קדשנו במצותיו וצונו להדליק נר של חנוכה.
- שעשה ניסים.
- שהחיינו.

On the following nights only the first two *brachos* are recited.

124. What if one forgot to say *shehecheyanu* on the first night?

If any of the lights are still burning he may still say *shehecheyanu*. If he remembered after all the lights had extinguished he should say *shehecheyanu* when lighting on the following night.

125. Does a mourner say *shehecheyanu*?

A mourner says *shehecheyanu* when he lights his own *menorah* at home. He should not light the *menorah* in shul on the first night when *shehecheyanu* is recited. (see question 169).

126. When should one begin to kindle the lights?

The lights should be kindled only after all the *brachos* have been recited.

127. May one speak while kindling the lights?

One should not speak until all the lights have been kindled unless the conversation concerns the *mitzvah*. Even this is forbidden if none of the lights has yet been kindled.

128. Should the *brachos* be repeated if a person spoke when lighting the *menorah*?

The *brachos* do not need to be repeated if a person spoke after one of the lights was already kindled. If he spoke before kindling any of the lights, he must repeat the *brachos*, unless the conversation concerned the *mitzvah*.

129. When should one say *HaNeros Hallalu*?

The main custom is to say it after the first light has been kindled, while kindling the remaining lights. Some wait until all the lights have been kindled.

130. What should be done if a person did not kindle enough lights?

If the lights are still burning he should correct the situation by kindling the appropriate number. The *brachos* are not repeated.

131. What should be done if a person lit too many lights?

He should extinguish the last redundant light(s).

132. May the *menorah* be moved after it has been lit?

Since the *mitzvah* is fulfilled at the moment of lighting, it is essential that the *menorah* be already situated in the correct position before it is lit. If the *menorah* was in an invalid place when kindled and was subsequently put in the correct place, the *mitzvah* has not been fulfilled. One should move the *menorah* to the correct place, repeat the *brachos*, and rekindle it.

133. May one move the lit *menorah* from one correct position to another?

Although both positions are suitable, one may not move the lit *menorah* until the lights have burned for the required time. To do so may give the impression that it was lit for personal use and not for the *mitzvah*.

It is preferable not to move it even after the required time, as long as the lights are still burning.

134. Must one remain by the lights for the first half-an-hour?

Strictly speaking this is not necessary since the *mitzvah* is fulfilled at the moment of lighting. However, some have the custom to remain by the lights whenever possible for the following reasons:

- To sing praises to *Hashem* and relate the miracles that occurred.
- To ensure that the ladies do not do work (see questions 13, 14).
- To rejoice in the miracle of the lights.

135. Why is it forbidden to benefit from the lights?

There are three reasons:

- To make it clear that they are *mitzvah* lights kindled solely for the purpose of publicizing the miracle.
- Since the miracle occurred with the *menorah* of the Temple, the lights are treated with the same holiness as the lights of the Temple *menorah*.
- So that a person does not become accustomed to degrade *mitzvos*.

136. What type of benefit is forbidden?

All personal benefit is forbidden. For example:
- Reading by their light.
- Eating a meal by their light.

- Lighting a candle from their flames.

137. May one eat a *seudas mitzvah* by the lights?

No.

138. May one learn Torah by the lights?

There are different opinions whether it is permitted to learn Torah by the light of the *menorah*. The widespread custom is not to.

139. May one light one *Chanukah* flame from another?

- If the *shamash* needs re-kindling, it may not be lit from one of the *Chanukah* lights.
- If a person wishes to rekindle an extinguished flame, the custom is to use the *shamash* and not one of the other *Chanukah* lights. Similarly, a second person who wishes to light his own *menorah* should take a light from the first person's *shamash*.

140. Doesn't the lighting of the *shamash* permit these benefits?

It is permitted to make use of the *shamash* when this does not involve using the *Chanukah* lights, e.g. to light a flame. However, one may not eat or read by the *menorah* since inevitably one will benefit from the *Chanukah* lights together with the *shamash*. Therefore, such activities are permitted only if another light is lit in the room.

Chapter Six – Lighting the Menorah

141. May one remain by the lit *menorah* if there is no other light in the room?

Although in this situation incidental benefit is inevitable (e.g. seeing one's way around the room), one may remain in the room. A person is not required to close his eyes.

142. May one benefit from the lights after half-an-hour?

It is preferable not to use the lights at any time, since an onlooker may not realize that they have already been burning for half-an-hour.

143. If oil remains in the *menorah* may it be reused the next evening?

Yes, this is permitted.

144. May one reuse the wicks the following evening?

See question 36.

145. If oil remains in the *menorah* after the eighth night may it be used for other purposes?

Since this oil was set aside for the *mitzvah* of *Chanukah*, it may not be used for anything else. It is even forbidden to use such oil for another *mitzvah* e.g. *Shabbos* lights.

146. What should be done with such oil?

It should be burned. The same applies to the used wicks after the eighth night.

147. Can this oil be saved for next *Chanukah*?

No, we are afraid that during the year it may accidentally be used for something else.

148. What about the leftover oil in the bottle?

This oil has not been designated for the *mitzvah* and may be used for any purpose.

Chapter Seven
Lighting Away from Home

149. Must one light the *menorah* at home?

The *mitzvah* of lighting the *menorah* is described as being 'a light for a man and his home'. From this we learn that the *mitzvah* is not only a personal one but also one that pertains to the home. Therefore a person cannot fulfill his obligation by lighting anywhere other than at home. For example, a man may not light at work but must return home for the *mitzvah* (see question 94).

150. When may a person light or become a partner at the home of a friend or relative?

Lighting or becoming a partner at another person's home is permitted only when sleeping at that place. A person, who intends to sleep the night at his own home, must light there and nowhere else. A boarder may be an exception to this rule (see questions 45, 46).

151. What if a person is away from home for part or all of *Chanukah* (e.g. on business) but his family remains at home?

The wife or son over bar mitzvah must light the *menorah* at home. Strictly speaking the husband also fulfills his obligation by this and is not required to light separately. However, according to the widespread custom, the husband lights his own *menorah* at the place where he is sleeping. He should make the *brachos* only if he lights earlier than the *menorah* is lit in his home. If he lights later than the *menorah* is lit in his home, he should not recite the *brachos* himself, but rather listen to someone else who is making the *brachos* wherever he is.

152. What if a woman is away from home during *Chanukah* but her husband is lighting at home?

The wife fulfills her obligation through her husband's lighting and is not required to light her own *menorah*. If possible she should try to hear the *brachos* being recited by someone else lighting wherever she is.

153. What if the wife is at home but the husband will arrive only later in the evening?

There are three options:
- The wife can wait for her husband to light the *menorah* when he arrives.
- The wife can light the *menorah* at the correct time and exempt the husband from lighting when he arrives.
- The husband can decide that he does not want to be exempted from lighting by his wife's lighting. She should light at the correct time and he should also light with the *brachos* when he arrives.

Chapter Seven – Lighting Away from Home

To avoid any misunderstanding, the couple should discuss the situation beforehand and come to a mutually acceptable arrangement.

154. What if the husband is at home but the wife will arrive only later in the evening?

If the wife agrees, the husband should light on time, thus fulfilling the obligation for himself and his wife. If the husband senses that his wife may be upset to miss the lighting of the *menorah*, he should wait until she arrives.

155. What if both the husband and wife go away together for a few days?

During the days that they are away from home, they should light the *menorah* in their new location. If any other members of the family remain at home they must light a *menorah* for themselves at home.

156. What should an unmarried person do when sleeping away from home?

A man should light his own *menorah* in the place he is lodging. A woman should become a partner with the family where she is lodging, but if she is lodging alone she must light her own *menorah* (see question 47 how to become a partner).

157. What if a person is sleeping away from home at one location and eating at another?

Preferably he should light at the place that he eats. If this is difficult, he may light where he sleeps.

158. Where should a person light on the day he leaves his home?

If he leaves before lighting time, he should light at his destination, but if he leaves after lighting time he should light at home before he leaves.

159. Where should a person light on the day he returns home?

If he leaves before lighting time he should light at home, but if he leaves after lighting time he should light at the place he has been temporarily.

160. Does the same apply to a person who returns home on *motzai Shabbos* after being away for *Shabbos*?

A person who intends to return home immediately after *Shabbos* should light when he arrives home. In this case, every effort should be made to return home quickly. A person who intends to remain at his temporary location for a while after *Shabbos* should light at the place he has been during *Shabbos*.

161. Where in a hotel should a guest light?

If permission is given he should light in his room since this is considered his home. It is praiseworthy to eat at least one meal a day in the room. If the hotel insists that he light in the communal dining room, he may fulfill his obligation there.

162. What if a person is travelling through the night?

- If he begins his journey after *plag haMincha*, he should light before he leaves.
- If he must leave before this time but will arrive at his destination before dawn, he should light when he arrives.
- If he must leave before this time and will arrive after dawn, he should light while travelling (see next question).

163. Under what conditions may one light when travelling?

One must fulfill several conditions:
- He is paying for the journey (e.g. train, boat, plane).
- He does not hold the *menorah* in his hand but puts it down somewhere.
- There is no fire hazard.

If **all** these conditions are met, he should light with *brachos*, even if he is able to light only one candle. If these conditions are not met, he is exempt from lighting.

164. What if he fears that he will have to extinguish the candle(s) within half-an-hour?

He should light without saying the *brachos*.

Chapter Eight

Lighting in Shul

165. Why is a *menorah* lit in shul?

A *menorah* is lit in shul in order to publicize the miracle.

166. Who fulfills his obligation by this lighting?

No one. The personal *mitzvah* can only be fulfilled by lighting a *menorah* at home. Even the person who lights the *menorah* is shul must light again at home.

167. Does this person repeat the *brachos* when lighting at home?

Yes. However, the *shehecheyanu b'racha* should not be repeated unless there are other members of the family who did not yet hear it and who are not lighting their own *menorah*.

168. If this person already lit at home may he recite the *brachos* again in shul?

Yes. Even the *shehecheyanu b'racha* is repeated in shul.

169. May a mourner light the *menorah* in shul?

He may light on any evening except the first. This is because the *shehecheyanu b'racha* should not be recited by a mourner on behalf of the congregation (see also question 125).

170. May a child light the *menorah* in shul?

No, this is not respectable for the congregation.

171. When should the shul *menorah* be lit?

Between *mincha* and *ma'ariv* when the congregation is assembled. Even in communities where individuals light after nightfall, the shul *menorah* is lit earlier. This is because people must hurry home after *ma'ariv* to light their own *menorah* and it would not be correct to delay them in shul. In *Eretz Yisrael* the custom is to light the *menorah* during *mincha*, before *aleinu*.

172. What if the shul does not have a *mincha* service but has one for *ma'ariv*?

The *menorah* should be lit before *ma'ariv* when a *minyan* is assembled. This is irrespective of the time of *ma'ariv*.

173. What if *ma'ariv* is *davened* many times in the same shul during the evening?

The *menorah* should be lit before the first *minyan*. If it is still burning for the later *minyanim* nothing needs to be done. If it was extinguished or went out by itself it should be re-lit without a *b'racha* by the next *minyan*.

174. For how long should the lights burn in shul?

They should burn for at least half-an-hour, but some communities use a large quantity of oil (or long candles) to enable the lights to burn late into the night. The reason is to resemble the *menorah* in the Temple, which burned through the entire night. If there is a fire risk the lights may be extinguished when everyone leaves shul.

175. Should the *menorah* be lit again before *shacharis*?

Some communities have a custom to re-light it without a *b'racha* before *shacharis*. This is the prevalent custom in *Eretz Yisrael*.

176. When should the *menorah* be lit on *erev Shabbos*?

Preferably between *mincha* and *ma'ariv* as usual, since this creates greater publicity. However, if *Shabbos* is approaching and there will not be sufficient time to light it after *mincha*, the *menorah* should be lit before *mincha*.

177. What if a *minyan* has not yet arrived when it is lit?

If possible one should wait for a *minyan* before lighting, but if this is difficult one may light with *brachos* even before a *minyan* has arrived.

Chapter Eight – Lighting in Shul

178. When should the *menorah* be lit on *Motzai Shabbos*?

It should be lit at the conclusion of *ma'ariv* after *kaddish tiskabel*. If the person who is lighting forgot to say אתה חוננתנו during *Shemoneh Esrei*, he should say ברוך המבדיל בין קודש לחול before lighting.

179. Where should the *menorah* be placed in shul?

- If the shul faces east or west, the *menorah* should be placed by the southern wall towards the front of the shul to resemble the *menorah* of the Temple, which was positioned at that side.
- If the shul faces south it should be placed by the front wall, preferably on the left side of the *aron kodesh*, so that the first light is close to the *aron kodesh*.
- If the shul faces north (i.e. it is south of Jerusalem), the southern wall is at the back of the shul. Therefore, the *menorah* should be placed by the left wall (west) in the first half of the shul (towards the south). Some have the custom to place it by the right wall (east).

180. Should it be hung on the wall?

It may be hung on the wall or placed on a table or shelf.

181. Should the lights be placed along an east-west line or a north-south line?

Preferably they should be on an east-west line.

182. How high should the *menorah* be?

As high as possible, so that it can be seen easily by everyone.

183. May one benefit from the lights of the shul *menorah*?

No.

184. May a *menorah* be lit at other public gatherings (e.g. weddings, rallies etc.)?

A *menorah* may be lit but *brachos* must not be recited. This is true even if there is a *minyan* for *ma'ariv* and even if some people present have not lit or seen a *menorah*.

Chapter Nine
Erev Shabbos

185. When should one *daven mincha* on *erev Shabbos*?

Preferably one should *daven mincha* before lighting the *menorah*. This is the same sequence of events as in the Temple, where the *menorah* was lit after the afternoon offering. If this is not possible one may *daven mincha* after lighting the *menorah*. According to some opinions, a special effort should be made to *daven mincha* before lighting when the first day of *Chanukah* is on *Shabbos*. This is because of a doubt if one should say *al haNissim* during the *mincha Shemoneh Esrei* once one has already lit the *menorah*. If this situation arises, one should not say *al haNissim*.

186. Is it preferable to *daven mincha* with a *minyan* after lighting the *menorah*, or to *daven* alone before lighting?

It is better to *daven* with a *minyan* after lighting.

187. When should the *menorah* be lit on *erev Shabbos*?

It should be lit before kindling the *Shabbos* lights.

188. Why is this the correct order?

When a person kindles the *Shabbos* lights he usually accepts *Shabbos* at that time and is forbidden to do any *melacha*. It would therefore be forbidden to light the *menorah* after the *Shabbos* lights.

189. What if one mistakenly kindled the *Shabbos* lights first?

A woman certainly may not kindle the *menorah* after the *Shabbos* lights since she has accepted *Shabbos*. A man who kindles *Shabbos* lights (e.g. lives alone, wife is away) usually does not accept *Shabbos* at that time. Therefore if he mistakenly kindled the *Shabbos* lights first he should light the *menorah* afterwards (provided it is still before sunset). If he had in mind to accept *Shabbos* when kindling the *Shabbos* lights, he too would be forbidden to light the *menorah*.

190. Is there any way to light the *menorah* after accepting *Shabbos*?

One may ask another person to light the *menorah* on his behalf, provided that the other person has not accepted *Shabbos* and it is still before sunset.

191. Who should recite the *brachos* in this situation?

The one who lights should recite the first *b'racha* (להדליק נר של חנוכה) and the owner of the *menorah* may recite the second *b'racha* and *shehecheyanu* on the first night.

192. Should the husband light the *menorah* before the wife kindles the *Shabbos* lights?

Yes. Since the *menorah* is lit also on behalf of the wife, it should be kindled before she accepts *Shabbos*.

193. Should the wife kindle the *Shabbos* lights only after all the *Chanukah* lights have been lit?

Ideally yes, but if time is short she may kindle the *Shabbos* lights as soon as the husband had kindled one *Chanukah* light.

194. If other *menorahs* are also to be lit (e.g. by children, visitors) should the wife wait until all have been lit?

No, she may kindle the *Shabbos* lights as soon as her husband has lit his *menorah*.

195. If the husband is not ready to light the *menorah* and time is short, may the wife kindle the *Shabbos* lights first?

Yes. The husband may still light the *menorah* afterwards, provided it is still before sunset. The same applies if the wife mistakenly kindled the *Shabbos* lights first.

196. What is the optimal time for lighting the *menorah* on *erev Shabbos*?

- The *Shabbos* lights should be lit at the usual time, preceded by the *Chanukah* lights.

- In Jerusalem, the custom throughout the year is to kindle the *Shabbos* lights forty minutes before sunset, but on *erev Shabbos Chanukah* they are lit twenty-five minutes before sunset after the lighting of the *menorah*. Some Jerusalem families kindle the *Shabbos* lights at the usual time, preceded by the *Chanukah* lights.

197. What is the earliest time for lighting the *menorah*?

The earliest time is *plag haMincha*. This is 1¼ seasonal hours before sunset. (In Jerusalem, *plag haMincha* during *Chanukah* is approximately 60 minutes before sunset.)

198. What if a person lit a *menorah* before this time?

He has not fulfilled his obligation. The *menorah* should be extinguished and re-lit at the correct time. The *brachos* must be repeated.

199. Until when must the lights burn?

The lights must be capable of burning until half-an-hour after nightfall. Therefore one must be especially careful on *erev Shabbos* to use sufficient oil or long candles that will burn until this time. If the *menorah* can only contain a small amount of oil or small candles, an alternative should be used on *erev Shabbos* (see question 25).

200. Must children also use long candles?

Yes. The standard *Chanukah* candles are too small for *erev Shabbos* and children must be given *Shabbos* candles instead.

201. Must all the lights burn this long?

Ideally, all the lights should be capable of burning for this length of time. In extenuating circumstances, it is sufficient to use one long candle or one larger cup of oil.

202. What if one or more of the lights go out?

- If it is still before sunset and he has not yet accepted *Shabbos*, he should re-light it without a *b'racha*.
- If he has accepted *Shabbos* he should ask another person who has not accepted *Shabbos* to light it for him.
- If it is already sunset, nothing can be done. The obligation has been fulfilled even if all the lights go out.

203. Where should the *menorah* be placed?

The *menorah* should be put in the usual position. However, extra care must be taken to avoid winds and draughts from doors and windows. It is forbidden on *Shabbos* to open a door or window that will cause a flame to go out or flicker significantly.

204. If one lights outside, may the *menorah* be brought indoors after all the lights have been extinguished?

No, the *menorah* is *muktzeh* and may not be moved. If a person is afraid that it may be stolen he should not use an expensive *menorah* on *erev Shabbos*. One may use simple cups for oil or line up a row of candles (see question 25).

205. If the *menorah* is placed on an object (e.g. chair, table) may the object be moved with the *menorah* on it?

No, the chair is also *muktzeh*.

206. If an item that is not *muktzeh* was also placed on the chair before *Shabbos*, can the chair be moved?

No, even in this situation the chair is *muktzeh* and cannot be moved.

207. May the *menorah* be brought inside in an unusual way?

Yes, one may hold it in an unusual way, e.g. between one's arms. This is permitted only if there is no prohibition of carrying, e.g. if there is an *eiruv*, or the *menorah* is inside a private enclosed yard.

Chapter Ten
Motzai Shabbos

208. Is the *menorah* lit on *motzai Shabbos* before or after *havdolah*?

The main custom is to make *havdolah* before lighting the *menorah*. Some have the custom to light the *menorah* first.

209. If a person has not yet made *havdolah* how can he do the *melacha* of lighting the *menorah*?

He must either *daven ma'ariv* first (where *havdolah* is included in the *Shemoneh Esrei*) or say the words ברוך המבדיל בין קודש לחול.

210. What is the optimal time for lighting?

Ideally, the *menorah* should be lit no later than half-an-hour after nightfall. For this reason, some congregations *daven ma'ariv* on *motzai Shabbos Chanukah* earlier than usual, to enable people to return home to light on time. If this time passed, one may still light with the *brachos*. In order to avoid unnecessary delay, sufficient lights should be prepared on *erev Shabbos* to use on *erev Shabbos* and on *motzai Shabbos*. Alternatively, the wife, after saying ברוך המבדיל בין קודש לחול, could prepare the *menorah* on *motzai Shabbos* for her husband to light upon his return from shul.

211. What if a person usually waits until the time of *Rabbeinu Tam* before doing any *melacha*?

A person who has firmly accepted this opinion should wait on *Chanukah* also. Otherwise, he should light at the same time as everyone else.

212. Can the *Chanukah* lights be used as the *havdolah* candle?

A person who lights the *menorah* first may not use the lights for *havdolah* since it is forbidden to benefit from the *Chanukah* lights, even for another *mitzvah* (see question 135).

213. May one use the *havdolah* candle for the *menorah*?

A standard *havdolah* candle that is made of several flames may not be used for the *menorah* since each *Chanukah* light must be a single flame. However, if a person makes *havdolah* using two individual candles held together, he may extinguish them and re-use them separately for the *Chanukah* lights. Indeed, it is praiseworthy to do so, since an object used for one *mitzvah* should be re-used for another *mitzvah*.

Chapter Eleven
Prayers on *Chanukah*

214. What are the main changes to the prayers on *Chanukah*?

- *Al haNissim* is added to the *Shemoneh Esrei* and *bensching*.
- Whole *hallel* is said.
- *Tachanun* and *lamnatzeach* are omitted.
- The Torah is read.

215. Where is *al haNissim* recited in *Shemoneh Esrei*?

It is said during *Modim*. The reason is that the entire festival of *Chanukah* is an expression of thanks to *Hashem* for the miracles that occurred.

216. Should one say על הניסים or ועל הניסים?

Both versions are acceptable. According to some opinions, 'ועל' is more correct.

217. May one recite *al haNissim* by heart?

Since this has not been said for an entire year, one must use a *siddur* at least the first time, in order to prevent mistakes.

218. What if one forgot to say it?

- If he has not yet said the name of *Hashem* at the conclusion of the *b'racha*, he should go back to *al haNissim* and continue on from there.
- If he has already said *Hashem's* name he should continue the *Shemoneh Esrei*. At the end of the paragraph נצור א-להי before saying the verse יהיו לרצון he should add a special prayer;

"יהי רצון מלפניך שתעשה לנו נסים ונפלאות כשם שעשית לאבותינו בימים ההם בזמן הזה".

He should then continue בימי מתתיהו.

219. What if he forgot to say this special prayer?

He does not repeat *Shemoneh Esrei*.

220. Is whole *hallel* said every day or only on the first day?

Whole *hallel* is said every day (including *rosh chodesh*). The reason is that a new miracle occurred with the oil every day.

221. Are women obligated to recite *hallel*?

- According to most opinions, women are exempt from saying *hallel* since it is a time-bound *mitzvah*.
- According to some opinions, *hallel* on *Chanukah* is an exception and should be recited by women. This is because women were included in the decrees and were instrumental in the miraculous defeat of the enemy (see also question 40 regarding the *menorah*).

Chapter Eleven – Prayers on Chanukah

222. Must *hallel* be said in the morning during *shacharis*?

Although it is preferable to recite *hallel* immediately after *Shemoneh Esrei*, it may be said all day until sunset if necessary.

223. Is a special daily psalm recited on *Chanukah*?

In many communities Psalm 30 (מזמור שיר חנוכת) is said after *shacharis*, as well as or instead of the usual daily psalm.

224. Where is *al haNissim* added to *bensching*?

In the second *b'racha*.

225. What if one forgot to say it?

- If he has not yet said the name of *Hashem* at the conclusion of the *b'racha*, he should go back to *al haNissim* and continue again from there.
- If he has already said the name of *Hashem* he should continue *bensching*. Upon reaching the special *haRachaman* prayers that are recited on *Shabbos* and *Yom Tov*, he should add a special prayer:

"הרחמן יעשה לנו נסים ונפלאות כשם שעשה לאבותינו בימים ההם בזמן הזה."

He should then continue בימי מתתיהו.

226. If one forgets *al haNissim* on *Shabbos* or *rosh chodesh*, where should the special *haRachaman* be inserted?

After the *haRachaman* for *Shabbos* or *rosh chodesh*.

227. What if he forgot the special *haRachaman*?

He does not repeat *bensching*. This is the case even on *Shabbos* and *rosh chodesh*.

228. If *Chanukah* begins on *motzai Shabbos* and *seuda shlishis* continues into the night, should one say *al haNissim* in *bensching*?

Since it would be a contradiction to recite both *retzei* and *al haNissim*, one should only say *retzei*.

229. Is *Chanukah* mentioned in the *b'racha* of *al haMichyah*?

No.

Glossary

Aleinu – Prayer recited at the conclusion of *shacharis*, *mincha* and *ma'ariv*.

Al haMichyah – *B'racha* recited after eating a *kezayis* of grain product, e.g. cake.

Aron kodesh – The holy ark in which the Torah scrolls are kept.

Ashkenaz – German or Polish Jewry.

B'racha (pl. *brachos*) – A blessing.

Bensch – To recite grace after meals.

Chashmonaim – Hasmoneans.

Cohanim – Priests.

Cohen Gadol – High priest.

Daven – To pray.

Dreidel – Four sided spinning top.

Eiruv – Enclosure of a public domain which transfers it into a private one in order to permit objects to be carried on *Shabbos*.

Halacha (pl. *halachos*) – Jewish law.

Hashem – G-d.

Havdolah – Prayer recited at the conclusion of *Shabbos* and *Yom Tov* to divide between a holy day and a weekday.

Hechsher – Rabbinical supervision.

Kaddish – Prayer that calls for the exaltation of G-d, recited by the leader of the service and by mourners.

Kaddish Tiskabel – The *kaddish* recited at the conclusion of the service.

Lamnatzeach – Psalm 20, recited towards the conclusion of *shacharis*.

Ma'ariv – The evening prayer.

Melacha – Type of constructive act that is forbidden on *Shabbos*.

Mezuzah (pl. *mezuzos*) – Parchment scroll on which parts of the Torah (including the *shema*) are written. The scroll is affixed to the doorway of every room.

Mincha – The afternoon prayer.

Minyan (pl. *minyanim*) – A quorum of men required for congregational prayer.

Mitzvah (pl. *Mitzvos*) – A commandment.

Mishkan – The Tabernacle that was built in the wilderness.

Muktzeh – An object of forbidden usage which may not be moved on *Shabbos*.

Mussaf – The additional service said on *Shabbos* and *Yom Tov*.

Perek – A chapter.

Rabbeinu Tam – Rabbi Yakov, grandson of *Rashi*, considered to be one of the greatest of the *ba'alei Tosfos*.

Rav – Rabbi.

Rosh chodesh – The first day of the new month.

Sephard – Spanish or eastern Jewry.

Sefer (pl. *Sefarim*) – Book.

Seudas Mitzvah – Meal eaten to celebrate a *mitzvah*, e.g. wedding, circumcision, redemption of the firstborn etc.

Shacharis – The morning service.

Shechina – The Divine presence.

Shehecheyanu – The blessing made to thank *Hashem*

for bringing us to the time when we can benefit from a new item or perform a new *mitzvah*.

Shemoneh Esrei – Supplication that forms a central part of formal prayer. On a weekday this contains 19 blessings.

Shiva – The week of mourning after the passing of a close relative.

Sh'loshim – The thirty day period after the passing of a close relative.

Shevi'is – Produce from the final year of the seven year agricultural cycle.

Siddur – Prayer book.

Tachanun – Prayer recited immediately following *Shemoneh Esrei*.

Tevilah – Immersion.

Tzaddik (pl. *Tzaddikim*) – Righteous individual.

Vilna Gaon – Rabbi *Eliahu* (1720-1797), Genius of Vilna and leader of Eastern European Jewry.

Yahrzeit – Hebrew date on which a person passed away.

Yom Tov – A festival.

Index

A

Al haNissim
    correct version 71
    forgot during *bensching*..73
    forgot during *Shemoneh Esrei*..72
    recite during *bensching* on *Shabbos*............................74
    recited by heart 71
    recited on *Chanukah* 71, 73

Apartment block
    where to light 32

B

Boarder
    lighting the *menorah*...24
    where to light the *menorah*...25
    who eats and sleeps at different places 24
    who eats and sleeps at one place 24

Brachos
    at home if recited in shul 58
    forgot *shehecheyanu*..47
    husband reciting if wife lighting 54
    in shul..58
    light only after reciting..47
    mourner reciting *shehecheyanu*......................................47
    spoke before lighting 47
    spoke during lighting 47
    when another person lights..64
    when to repeat 48
    which to recite 46

C

Chanukah
    eating festive meals 14, 15
    giving money to children..16
    mentioned during *al haMichyah*.....................................74
    origin..13
    torah study..16
    travel during...20
    visiting cemetery...18

Index

Children
- lighting the *menorah* 24
- lighting the *menorah* in shul 59
- long candles on *erev Shabbos* 67

D

Doughnuts
- which *b'racha* 17
- which *b'racha* as a dessert 18

E

Eating
- doughnuts 17
- festive meals 14, 15
- foods fried in oil 15
- milk dishes 15

F

Fasting
- on *Chanukah* 16

G

Girls
- lighting in a seminary 26
- lighting the *menorah* 23, 25, 27

Greeks
- their decrees 13, 14, 15, 16

H

Hallel
- ideal time to recite 73
- recited during *Chanukah* 72

Havdolah
- *menorah* lit before or after 69
- using *menorah* as *havdolah* candle 70

Hotel
- where to light 56

L

Latkes
- which *b'racha* 17

Lighting
- after *mincha* on *erev Shabbos* 63
- earliest time 66
- eating or drinking before 39
- forgot *shehecheyanu* 47
- if sleeping and eating at different locations 55
- make *brachos* 46
- on day of travel 56
- sleeping before 40
- when travelling 57
- working before 38

Lights
- amount kindled 43
- extinguish 41
- forbidden to benefit from 49, 51
- kindle one flame from another 50
- kindled insufficient 48
- kindled too many 48
- length of time to burn 40
- not catch fire 42
- remain by after lighting 49
- types of forbidden benefit 49
- wind blew out 42

M

Menorah
- above 20 *amos* 34
- becoming a partner in 25
- *brachos* if lighting late 37
- carefully positioned on *erev Shabbos* 67
- correct height 30, 33
- *davening ma'ariv* before lighting 36
- distance between branches 19
- earliest time to light 37
- electric lights 22
- forbidden materals 19
- garden between door and street 29
- garden without doorframe 29
- ideal height in shul 62
- ideal time to light 37
- in apartment block 31
- in shul during *shacharis* 60
- latest time to light 37

Index

lighting after *Shabbos* lights 64
lighting at home..53
lighting at sunset or nightfall 36
lit at public gatherings 62
lit before *Shabbos* lights 63, 65
many people lighting by one entrance...................................32
many people lighting by one window 34
maximum publicity when lighting..46
move after lighting..48
moving inside on *Shabbos* 68
oil or candles 20, 43
one per household 23
outside a door facing the street 28
place inside glass case..28
placing for maximum publicity 31, 33
placing in doorway...30
placing in frosted window 34
placing in window 32, 33, 34
placing opposite *mezuzah*...29
preferable materals 19
preferable shape 19
publicizing miracle to gentiles...35
reward for fulfilling *mitzvah*...39
wait for *minyan* before lighting in shul 60
when to light in shul..59
where to light in *chutz la'aretz*...28
where to light in shul...61
which end to light 43, 44
why lit in shul 58
working before lighting...38

Mourner
festive meals 15
recite *brachos* in shul 58
reciting *shehecheyanu*...47
visiting cemetery during *Chanukah* 18

O

Oil
bitter tasting..21
insufficient before lighting...41
left under a bed 21
leftover in bottle 52
requires a *hechsher*..21
solidified 20
use the remainder for other purposes 51

Olive oil
 use the remainder the next night 51
 which to use 20
Olive oil
 preferred type of oil 20

P

Playing
 with cards 15
 with the *dreidel* 16

S

Seminary
 who has to light 26
Shabbos
 ideal time to light *motzai Shabbos* 69
 ideal time to light on *erev Shabbos* 65, 66
 moving *menorah* 68
 where to light if away 56
Shamash
 benefits of lighting 50
 light from other flames 50
 oil or wax 45
 one for each *menorah* 46
 when to light 45
 where to place 46
 why it is required 44
Shehecheyanu
 forgot on first night 47
 mourner reciting 47

T

Torah
 learning by the lights 50
Travel
 during *Chanukah* 20
 lighting during 57
 where to light 56

W

Wicks
 coated with wax 21

how to dispose of 22
  reuse the next night 21, 51
  which material to use 21
Women
  included in husbands lighting 24, 54, 55
  lighting on behalf of husband 24, 53, 54
  lighting the *menorah* 23
  obligation to recite *hallel* 72
  refraining from work 17
  restrictions before lighting..40

Y

Yeshivah
  lighting at home or in dormitory 35
  lighting in dormitory 35
  who has to light 26

Hebrew Sources

[1] רמב"ם הל' חנוכה פ"א, ה"א, מ"ב ריש ס' תרע. [2] רמב"ם פ"א ה"ב, ג, מ"ב שם. [3] מ"ב שם, רמ"א סע' ב, מ"ב סק"ז. [4] ס' תרפג-תרפד. [5] מ"ב ס' תרע סק"ו. [6] רמ"א סע' ב, מ"ב סק"ט, וביה"ל. [7] מבקשי תורה ס' רב אות כח בשם הגרשז"א זצ"ל. [8] מנהג ישראל תורה ס' תרע סע' ג. [9] רמ"א סע' ב, מ"ב סק"י. [10] סע' א, רמ"א סע' ג, ערוה"ש סק"ז. [11] פסקי תשובות אות ד הע' 26. [12] מ"ב סס"ק"א, קצש"ע ס' קלט ססי"א, מג"א ריש סימן תרע, יסוד ושורש העבודה שער יב, פ"א, פרמ"ג א"א ריש ס' תרע. [13] סע' א, מ"ב סק"ג. [14] מ"ב סק"ג. [15] הליכות בת ישראל פכ"א ס"ק לד. [16] רמ"א ס' רח סע' ח, מ"ב ס"ק לח, מחבר סע' ב, מ"ב סק"ז, וע' בספר וזאת הברכה. [17] מ"ב ס' קסח ס"ק פב. [18] שם, פסקי הלכות של הגר"נ קרליץ עמ' כט וע' חזו"א ס' כו סק"ב, ג שפסק לקולא. [19] וזאת הברכה, בירור הלכה ס' יב, ע"פ בה"ל ד"ה וירא. [20] ע' גשר החיים פכ"ט ס' ו, ותשובות והנהגות ח"ב ס' סה. [21] מ"ב ס' תרעג סע"ב כח, כף החיים ס' תרעג סק"ס. [22] שע"ת סו"ס תרעג, כף החיים ס"ק סא. [23] ביה"ל ס' תרעא סע' ד ד"ה מילא, חיי אדם כלל קנד סע' י, מבית לוי להגר"ש ואזנר ח"י עמ' יב. [24] מ"ב ס' תרעא ס"ק יח, מבית לוי להגר"ש ואזנר ח"י עמ' יג. [25] שבה"ל ח"ח ס' קנז. [26] פשוט. [27] מ"ב ס' תרעג סק"ד. [28] ס' תרעג סע' א. [29] מ"ב סק"ב, ערוה"ש סק"א. [30] מבית לוי להגר"ש ואזנר ח"י עמ' יג/יד, ערוה"ש ס' תרעג סע' א, ובפסקי ר' ניסים קרליץ פ"ח עמ' כז מסתפק בזה. [31] מבית לוי להגר"ש ואזנר ח"י, עמ' יד, מבקשי תורה ס' רא אות ה בשם הגרשז"א זצ"ל. [32] דנו הפוסקים לגבי שמן של בו"ח, ערלה, טבל ושביעית. ע' מ"ב סק"ב, שערי תשובה ס' תקעג סק"א, אג"מ ח"א ס' קצא, מנחת יצחק ח"ז ס' מז, פאת השולחן פ"ה סע' ט בבית הרידב"ז, שו"ת אמרי יושר ח"א ס' ק. [33] חזו"א דמאי ס' טו סק"א, שמועה בשם הגרי"ש"א. [34] כה"ח ס' תרעג ס"ק יא, וע"ע מרחשת ח"א ס' כ. [35] מ"ב ס' תרעג סק"ב. [36] ס' תרעג סע' ד, מ"ב ס"ק לא, מאירי שבת כא/א ד"ה זה שביארנו בא"ד. [37]

[38] שו"ת הר צבי קש"ע ס' קלט סע' כ, מ"ב ס' כא סק"ו. [39] ס' תרעא סע' ח"ב ס' קיד, ציץ אליעזר ח"א ס' כ פי"ב. [40] ס' תרעה סע' ג, מ"ב סק"ט, י. [41] מ"ב ס' ב ורמ"א. [42] רמ"א ס' תרעה סע' ג ומ"ב ס"ק יד, מ"ב תרעה סק"ט, חתם סופר שבת דף כא ד"ה והמהדרין, מ"ב ס' תרעה סק"ט. [43] מ"ב ס' תרעה ס' תרעז ס"ק יג, חנוך לנער ס' כו סק"א. סק"ט. [44] מ"ב ס' תרעז סק"א. [45] מ"ב שם וסק"ג, שעה"צ סק"י, הליכות בת ישראל פכ"א, סע' ז. [46] מ"ב ס' תרעז ס"ק יב. [47] מ"ב סק"ג, שעה"צ סק"ט. [48] מ"ב שם. [49] ביה"ל ד"ה להשתתף וכו'. [50] חובת הדר פ"א ס"ק נט ד"ה ועתה, מ"ב סק"א. [51] חובת הדר שם, הליכות בת ישראל פכ"א סע' ח. [52] ס' תרעה סק"ט, ס' תרעז סק"ד. [53] נחלקו הראשונים אם יש חיוב הגוף בנר חנוכה, ונפסקו שתי הדיעות במחבר (ס' תרעו סע' ג וס' תרעז, סע' ג). ולכאורה כדי לצאת ידי המחלקת צריך לשמוע הברכות מאחר (פסק"ת ס' תרעה סע' ג). [54] ביה"ל ס' תרעז סע' א ד"ה עמו וכו'. [55] ס' תרעא סע' ה. [56] דרכי משה סק"ט, ערוה"ש ס"ק כד, מנח"י ח"ו ס' סו. [57] שו"ת שאילת יעב"ץ ח"א ס' קמט, הובא בשע"ת סוס"י תרעג, מנח"י הנ"ל, וע"ע בערוה"ש הנ"ל. [58] ס' תרעא סע ה, גרי"ז, חזו"א או"ח ס' סה, נב; יו"ד ס' קסח סק"ו. [59] שבות יצחק הל' חנוכה פ"א אות ג בשם הגרישו"א. [60] ס' תרעא סע' ז. [61] שם. [62] מ"ב ס"ק לג. [63] מחבר שם, מ"ב ס"ק לו. [64] מ"ב ס' תרעו סק"ט. [65] ס' תרעא סע' ו, מ"ב ס"ק כז. [66] שעה"צ סק"ל. [67] הגרח"ק הובא בקונטרס הלכות חנוכה ס' ד, אות כט, ע"פ שעה"צ הנ"ל. [68] חובת הדר פ"א ס"ק יד, דיני חנוכה עמ' נד, ד. [69] מנחת יצחק ח"ז ס' מח. [70] ס' תרעא סע' ה, קונטרס ימי החנוכה עמ' קב בשם הגר"נ קרליץ. [71] שו"ת אז נדברו ח"ה ס' לט, וע"ע ארחות רבינו ח"ג עמ' יב אות לא. [72] הגרשז"א זצ"ל במבקשי תורה ס' רב אות א. [73] הגר"נ קרליץ שליט"א בסדר הדלקת נרות חנוכה, עמ' טו. [74] ע' מקורות 68, 70, 56, 73. [75] מ"ב ס' תרעא סק"ק לח, אג"מ או"ח ח"ד ס' קכבה. [76] ארחות רבינו ח"ג עמ' יב אות לא, קובץ על יד בשם הגרשז"א, הובא בדיני חנוכה (הוצאת דגל

ההלכה). [77] מ"ב ס' תרעא סק"ז כז. [78] ס' תרעא סע' ו, פרמ"ג מש"ז סק"ה, שבה"ל ח"ד ס' סה, הגרי"מ שטרן בספרו מועדי שנה (עמ' רנו), הגר"ש איידר, והגרש"א פוסל ע"פ השעה"צ ס"ק מב. [79] מבקשי תורה ס' רב אות ז בשם הגרשז"א זצ"ל. [80] מבקשי תורה בשם הגרי"ש שליט"א, מבית לוי להגר"ש ואוזנר ח"י עמ' ו. [81] ס' תרעא, רמ"א סע' ב וסע' ז. [82] אג"מ ח"ד ס' קה אות ז (אין פר"ן), הגריש"א הובא בשבות יצחק סוף פ"ב (יש פר"ן), וע' פסקי תשובות ס' תרעא אות ו, מבקשי תורה ס' רב, אות י בשם הגרשז"א זצ"ל. [83] מבקשי תורה ס' רב אות כ בשם הגרשז"א זצ"ל. [84] לדעת האג"מ יו"ד ח"ג ס' יד (ה), או"ח ח"ד ס' ע (ג), שבה"ל ח"ג ס' פג, מנח"י ח"ז ס' מח, תשובות והנהגות ח"ב ס' שמב (יא), להורות נתן ח"ו ס' מד, חדר שינה עדיף; לדעת הגר"א קוטלר והחזו"א (הובאו בתשובות והנהגות שם) חדר אוכל עדיף; לדעת הגריש"א הובא בשבות יצחק הל' חנוכה פ"ו אות ד פתח הבנין בו הם ישנים עדיף. [85] מ"ב ס' תרעב סק"א, ביה"ל ד"ה עם סוף השקיעה, מעשה רב אות רלה, אג"מ או"ח ח"ד ס' קא (ו), חזו"א הובא בשבות יצחק עמ' עב, הגר"א קוטלר הובא בהלכות חנוכה של הגר"ש איידר עמ' 20, הערה ו. [86] מ"ב שם, ביה"ל ד"ה לא מאחרין, ס' תרעז סס"ק טז. [87] מבית לוי להגר"ש ואוזנר ח"י עמוד א, הליכות שלמה פ"ב הערה 62, אג"מ או"ח ח"ד ס' צט. [88] ס' תרעב סע' ב. [89] מ"ב ס"ק יא, שעה"צ ס"ק יז. [90] מ"ב הנ"ל, וע' שעה"צ הנ"ל שהמברך יש על מי לסמוך, וכן המנהג, שבה"ל ח"ח ס' קנו, מבקשי תורה ס' רב אות י בשם הגרשז"א זצ"ל, אג"מ או"ח ח"ד ס' קה (ז). [91] סוס"ע ב, מ"ב ס"ק יב. [92] מ"ב ס' תרעב סק"ג. [93] שבה"ל ח"ד ס' סו. [94] מ"ב ס' תרעב סק"י, שגם שאר דברים אסורים וכגון מסחר, שעב"צ ס"ק יד. [95] תשובות והנהגות ח"א ס' שצ, רמ"א ס' תרעב סע' ב, מ"ב ס' תרעא סק"א. [96] שעה"צ ס' תרעב ס"ק יד. [97] מ"ב ס' רלב סק"ט, ביה"ל ד"ה לבורסקי, ס' תרעב סק"י. [98] שעה"צ ס' תרעב ס"ק יד. [99] מ"ב ס' רלב ס"ק לה, ס' תלא סק"ו. [100] מ"ב ס' תרעב סק"י, ס' רלה ס"ק יז. [101] כן נראה ע"פ מ"ב הנ"ל, וע' אשי ישראל

פכ"ז סק"ס וס"ק פ"ז.   [102] מבית לוי להגר"ש ואזנר ח"י עמ' כב.   [103] מחבר סע' ב, מ"ב סק"ה, ו, לפי יסוד תשובות והנהגות ה"א ס' שץ שזמן תכלה רגל מן השוק האריך הזה"ז.   [104] מועדים וזמנים ח"ח ס' קמא, הגרי"ז הובא בשבות יצחק עמ' עט, והגריי"ק הקפיד שידליקו עד חצי שעה אחרי צה"כ של ר"ת, מ"ב סק"ו.   [105] מחבר סע' ב, מ"ב סק"ז.   [106] ס' תרעג סע' א, מ"ב ס"ק כז.   [107] ס' תרעה סע' ב, מ"ב סק"ח.   [108] מ"ב ס' תרעג ס"ק כה, שעה"צ סק"ל.   [109] מ"ב שם.   [110] ס' תרעג סע' ב, מ"ב ס"ק כז.   [111] ס' תרעא סע' ב, מ"ב סק"ד.   [112] מ"ב שם.   [113] מ"ב סק"ז.   [114] ס' תרעו סע' ב, מ"ב סק"ט.   [115] שם וס"ק יא.   [116] מ"ב ס"ק יא, שעה"צ ס"ק יט.   [117] ס' תרעג סע' א.   [118] שם וברמ"א.   [119] שם, מבית לוי להגר"ש ואזנר ח"י עמ' טו.   [120] שם ובמ"ב ס"ק טז, כ.   [121] מ"ב ס"ק יח.   [122] ס' תרעה סק"ט, חיי"א כלל קנד סע' כ, מ"ב ס' תרעב סק"י.   [123] ס' תרעו סע' א, ב.   [124] מ"ב סק"ב, ד.   [125] מ"ב ס"ק מד.   [126] רמ"א סע' ב.   [127] ס' תלב סע' א.   [128] מ"ב שם סק"ה, ו, ס' תרעב סק"ו.   [129] מ"ב ס' תרעו סק"ח.   [130] מ"ב ס' תרעב סק"ו.   [131] פשוט.   [132] ס' תרעה סע' א, מ"ב סק"ה.   [133] מ"ב סק"ו, שעה"צ ס' תקעב ס"ק יב.   [134] מבקשי תורה ס' רא סע' ג בשם הגרשז"א זצ"ל, יסוד ושורש העבודה שער יב, פ"א בא"ד ד"ה ותכף, תשובות והנהגות ח"א ס' שצד.   [135] מ"ב ס' תרעג סק"ח, י"א.   [136] ס' תרעג סע' א, ס' תרעד סע' א.   [137] מ"ב ס' תרעג סק"ט.   [138] מ"ב ס"ק יב.   [139] רמ"א ס' תרעד סע' א.   [140] מ"ב ס' תרעג ס"ק טו.   [141] מ"ב ס' תרעג ס"ק יא, שעה"צ ס"ק יא.   [142] מ"ב ס' תרעב סק"ח.   [143] מ"ב ס' תרעז ס"ק יז.   [144] עיין מקורות 36.   [145] ס' תרעז סע' ד.   [146] שם, קצש"ע ס' קלט סע' כ.   [147] מ"ב ס"ק יט.   [148] ביה"ל ד"ה הצריך וכו'.   [149] שבת כא: מ"ב ס' תרעז ס"ק יב.   [150] מ"ב שם.   [151] מ"ב ס' תרעז סק"ב, טז.   [152] שם.   [153] להגר"מ פיינשטיין הובא בהלכות חנוכה של הגר"ש איידר עמ' 35 הע' כב, ולהגרח"פ שייננבערג הובא בקונטרס הלכות חנוכה עמ' לז, ולהגר"ש ואזנר ח"ד ס' סו עדיף ע"י עצמו מאוחר;

ולהגרי"ש אלישיב ולהגרשז"א הובאו בקונטרס הלכות חנוכה עמ' מא עדיף ע"י שליח בזמן. ומ"מ שלום בית עדיף מן הכל. [154] כנ"ל. [155] ביה"ל ס' תרעז סע' א ד"ה במקום. [156] מ"ב ס' תרעז סק"א, ז. [157] ס' תרעז סע' א ברמ"א, מ"ב ס"ק יא, יב, מבית לוי להגר"ש ואזנר ח"י עמ' י. [158] שבה"ל ח"ה ס' קנח. [159] שם. [160] מבקשי תורה ס' רב אות כד בשם הגרשז"א. [161] חובת הדר פ"ב סע' ט, מקורות 84. [162] שו"ת משנה הלכות ח"ז ס' פו, שו"ת שבט הלוי ח"ח ס' קנח. [163] שו"ת מהרש"ם ח"ד ס' קמו, ערוה"ש ס' תרעז סע' ה. [164] פסקי תשובות אות ג. [165] ס' תרעא סע' ז. [166] רמ"א שם, מ"ב ס"ק מה. [167] מ"ב שם. [168] שערי תשובה סק"ז. [169] מ"ב ס"ק מד. [170] מנחת יצחק ח"ו, ס' סה (א), מבית לוי להגר"ש ואזנר ח"י עמ' יז. [171] רמ"א שם, מ"ב ס"ק מו, לוח א"י. [172] שו"ת משנה שכיר ס' רב. [173] מבית לוי להגר"ש ואזנר ח"י עמ' יט. [174] מ"ב ס' תרעה סק"ו, מג"א ס' תרע סק"ב, שבה"ל ח"ח ס' קנו. [175] פרמ"ג א"א ס' תרע סק"ב, לוח א"י. [176] רמ"א שם, מ"ב ס"ק מז. [177] ביה"ל ד"ה ויש נוהגין. [178] ס' תרפא סע' ב, לוח א"י, מ"ב סק"ב. [179] ס' תרעא סע' ז, מ"ב סק"מ, שו"ת בצל החכמה ח"ב ס' נ, פסקי הלכות של הגר"נ קרליץ עמ' טז. [180] מ"ב שם. [181] רמ"א שם מ"ב ס"ק מב. [182] ס' תרעא מ"ב ס"ק כז. [183] מ"ב ס' תרעג ס"ק יג. [184] שבה"ל ח"ד ס' סה, מנח"י ח"ו ס' סה (ג). [185] מ"ב סו"ס תרעט, שערי תשובה שם, הליכות שלמה פט"ז, סע' כה. [186] כה"ח ס' תרעא ס"ק עט. [187] ס' תרעט סע' א. [188] מ"ב סק"א. [189] שם. [190] שם. [191] שם. [192] בנין שלמה ס' נג. [193] בן איש חי שנה א פ' וישב הל' חנוכה אות כ. [194] פשוט. [195] פשוט. [196] אג"מ או"ח ח"ד ס' סב, מועדים וזמנים ח"ו ס' פד בשם הגרי"ז, מבקשי תורה ס' רב אות יב בשם הגרשז"א זצ"ל, לוח א"י. [197] מ"ב סק"ב. [199] שם. [200] פשוט. [201] מ"ב סק"ב. [202] ס' תרעג סע' ב, מ"ב ס"ק כו, כז. [203] מ"ב ס' תרפ סק"א, ב, ג, ד, וע' ששכ"כ פי"ג סע' לג. [204] ס' רעט סע' א. [205] ס' שי סע' ז. [206] שבות יצחק הל' מוקצה פט"ז אות י בשם הגרישז"א.

[207] מ"ב ס' רעו ס"ק לא.   [208] מ"ב סו"ס תרפא, ערוה"ש סע' ב, קצש"ע ס' קלט סע' יח.   [209] מ"ב סק"ב.   [210] מעשה רב אות רלז, לוח א"י.   [211] שבות יצחק עמוד עה בשם הגרשז"א והגריש"א, שתלוי אם נוהג כך מעיקר הדין או מחומרא.   [212] ס' תרפא סע' א.   [213] מ"ב סק"א, ס' תרעא ס"ק יד.   [214] ס' תרפב-תרפד.   [215] ס' תרפב סע' א, מ"ב סק"ב.   [216] מ"ב סק"א, יסוד ושורש העבודה שער יב, פ"א בא"ד ד"ה כתוב בספרים.   [217] מ"ב ס' ק סק"א .   [218] ס' תרפב סע' א, מ"ב סק"ד.   [219] מחבר שם.   [220] ס' תרפג ובמ"ב.   [221] מג"א ס' תכב סק"ה, שבה"ל ח"א ס' רה (ס' תרפג), אשי ישראל פמ"ח סע' יא.   [222] ביה"ל ס' תכב סע' ב ד"ה וקורין.   [223] לוח א"י.   [224] ס' תרפב סע' א.   [225] ס' תרפב סע' א וברמ"א.   [226] מ"ב סק"ה.   [227] מ"ב סק"ג.   [228] מ"ב ס' קפח ס"ק לג.   [229] מ"ב ס' תרפב סק"ב.

Dedicated in Memory of

ר׳ אליהו חיים בן
ר׳ דוד חייו ז״ל

ת.נ.צ.ב.ה.

נתרם בעילום שם

יהי רצון שיזכו

לברכה והצלחה

בכל מעשה ידיהם

לע"נ

**מרת צ'פא בילא בת
ר' מרדכי דוד ע"ה**

**ר' יצחק צבי בן
ר' מרדכי דוד ז"ל**

ଓ ଅ

לע"נ

ר' שלמה ב"ר משה ז"ל

**מרת רייזל דבורה בת
ר' יעקב מרדכי ע"ה**

ר' יצחק ב"ר זאב ז"ל

לע"נ

**מרת פייגע רבקה בת
ר' כתריאל דוד ע"ה**

ר' יעקב ב"ר מרדכי יוסף ז"ל

ת.נ.צ.ב.ה.

ೞ ೫

לע"נ

ר' יצחק ב"ר שמואל זנוויל ז"ל

ೞ ೫

לע"נ

ר' זלמן פסח ב"ר אברהם ז"ל

ר' שמואל אברהם ב"ר יעקב ז"ל